FRANCE

Tom Streissguth

Lerner Publications Company • Minneapolis

Copyright © 2009 by Lerner Publishing Group, Inc.

All rights reserved. International copyright secured. No part of this book may be reproduced, stored in a retrieval system, or transmitted in any form or by any means—electronic, mechanical, photocopying, recording, or otherwise—without the prior written permission of Lerner Publishing Group, Inc., except for the inclusion of brief quotations in an acknowledged review.

Lerner Publications Company
A division of Lerner Publishing Group, Inc.
241 First Avenue North
Minneapolis, MN 55401 U.S.A.

Website address: www.lernerbooks.com

Library of Congress Cataloging-in-Publication Data

Streissguth, Thomas, 1958–
    France / by Tom Streissguth.
      p.   cm. — (Country explorers)
    Includes index.
    ISBN: 978–0–8225–9412–3 (lib. bdg. : alk. paper) 1. France—Geography—Juvenile literature. 2. France—Description and travel—Juvenile literature. 3. France—Social life and customs—Juvenile literature. I. Title.
DC20.7.S77 2009
944—dc22
                                                    2007038877

Manufactured in the United States of America
1 2 3 4 5 6 – PA – 14 13 12 11 10 09

Table of Contents

Welcome!	4	School	30
The Land	6	Faiths of France	32
Paris	8	Let's Celebrate!	34
Traveling	10	Vacation	36
The People	12	On Your Bikes!	38
Famously French	14	Story Time	40
Sharing Words	16	Art	42
Cities and Towns	18	*The Flag of France*	*44*
Homes	20	*Fast Facts*	*45*
Family	22	*Glossary*	*46*
Food	24	*To Learn More*	*47*
And More Food!	26	*Index*	*48*
Shopping	28		

Welcome!

France lies on the continent of Europe. France is the second-biggest country in Europe.

France has six sides. Three sides touch water. They border the English Channel, the Atlantic Ocean, and the Mediterranean Sea. On the other three sides, France touches the countries of Spain, Italy, Switzerland, Germany, Luxembourg, and Belgium.

The island of Corsica lies in the Mediterranean Sea. It is part of France.

ATLANTIC OCEAN

The Land

Much of France's land is rolling hills. But France also has two high sets of mountains. They are the Alps and the Pyrenees. An area of smaller mountains and plateaus covers part of southern France. It is called the Massif Central.

Melted snow forms a beautiful lake in the Alps.

Several rivers flow through France. The longest is the Loire (LWAHR) River. The Seine (SAYN) is another important river. It flows through Paris.

Canals

Canals are waterways dug by people. Canals link France's biggest rivers to one another. Ships do not use these waterways anymore. But small boats float along the canals. Boaters enjoy views of the countryside.

In Paris, roads and buildings line the banks of the Seine.

Paris

Paris is the capital of France. It is also the largest city in the country. Paris spreads out on both sides of the Seine River. Life in Paris moves fast.

The city of Paris lights up at night. Can you see the Eiffel Tower?

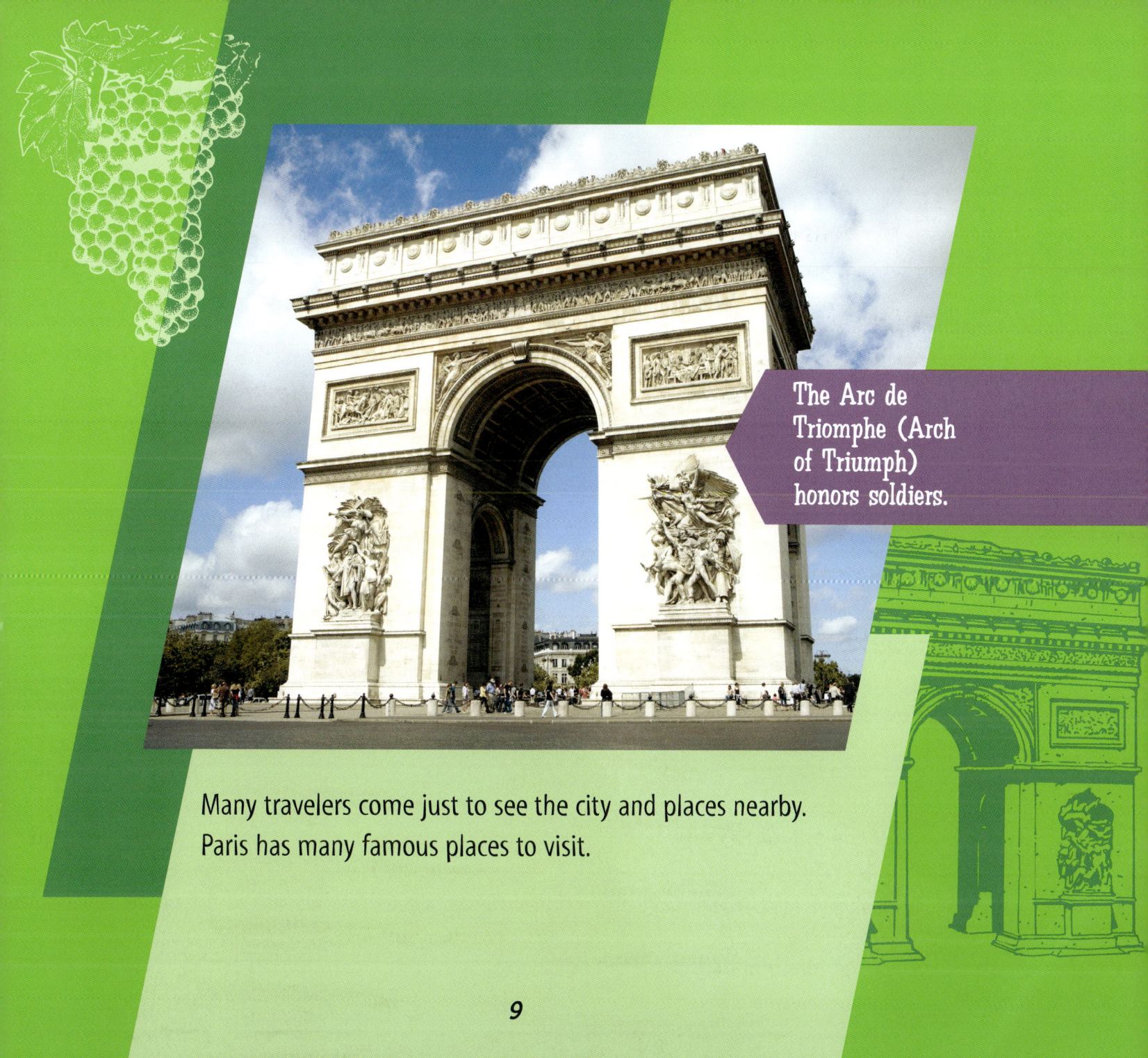

The Arc de Triomphe (Arch of Triumph) honors soldiers.

Many travelers come just to see the city and places nearby. Paris has many famous places to visit.

Traveling

French drivers go fast on the big highways. But in small towns, traffic slows down. The roads are narrow. Two cars can barely squeeze past each other.

This street is so narrow that cars cannot use it. The street lies in the village of Eze.

Many people who live in cities do not own a car. If they want to go somewhere, they hop on a train. One kind of train moves at very high speeds. It can travel 200 miles (322 kilometers) per hour!

Map Whiz Quiz

Take a look at the map on page 5. Trace the outline of France onto a sheet of paper. Can you find the Atlantic Ocean? Mark this side of your map with a *W* for west. Do you see the Mediterranean Sea? Mark it with an *S* for south. How about Switzerland? Mark this side with an *E* for east. Then look for the English Channel. Mark your map with an *N* for north. Color in the areas labeled the Alps and the Pyrenees.

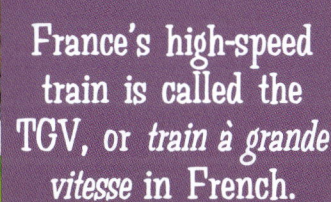

France's high-speed train is called the TGV, or *train à grande vitesse* in French.

Basque people celebrate their unique language and culture. Their ancestors lived in parts of modern-day France and Spain.

The People

Long ago, parts of France were ruled by different groups of Europeans. Many French people have ancestors that belonged to these groups. Their families have been in France for hundreds of years!

Other French citizens have parents or grandparents that moved to France from North Africa, Asia, or other parts of Europe. This is part of the reason French people do not always look alike. Sometimes there is conflict between these groups.

People from India watch a parade in Paris. The parade is part of a Hindu holiday festival.

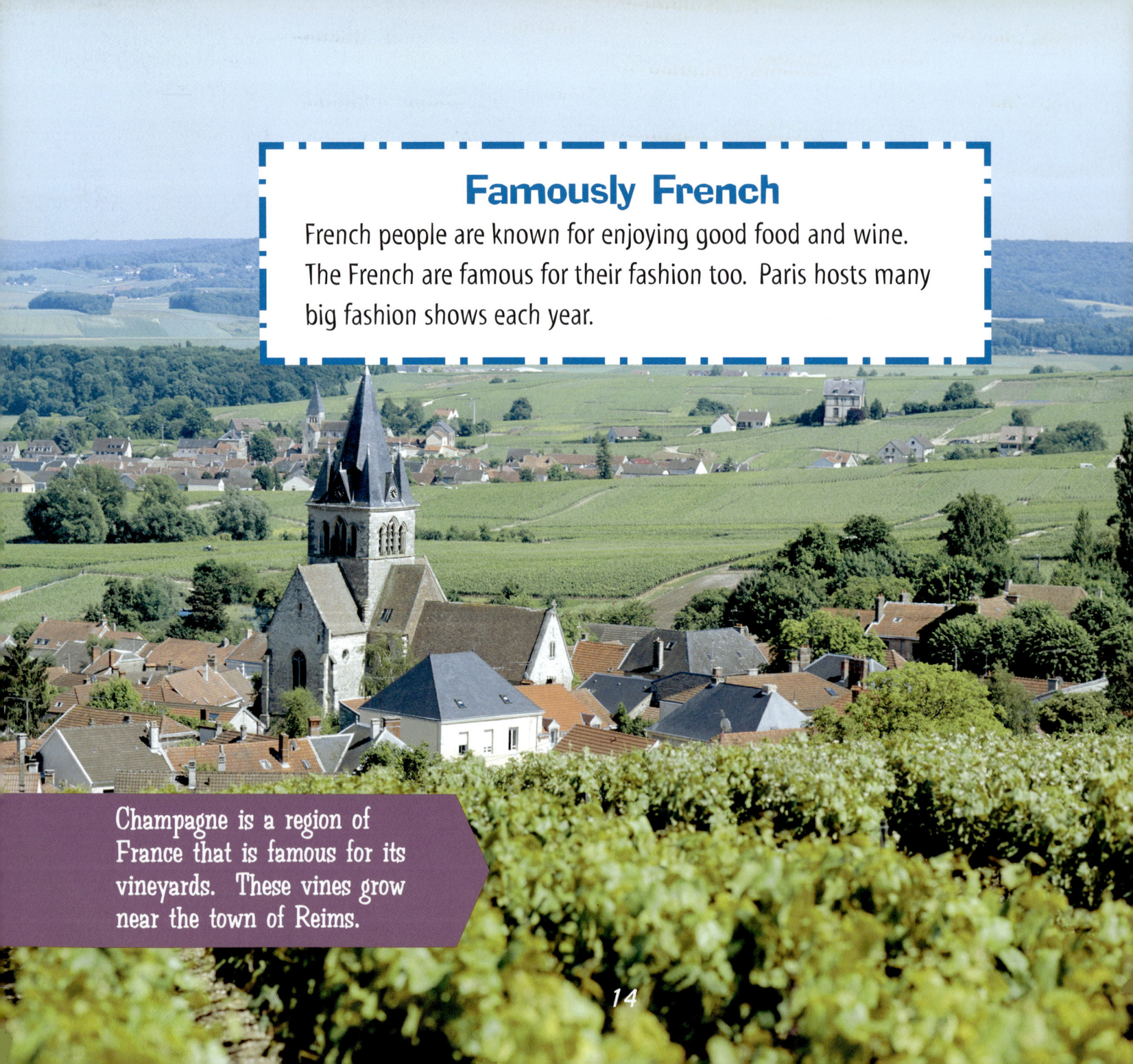

Famously French

French people are known for enjoying good food and wine. The French are famous for their fashion too. Paris hosts many big fashion shows each year.

Champagne is a region of France that is famous for its vineyards. These vines grow near the town of Reims.

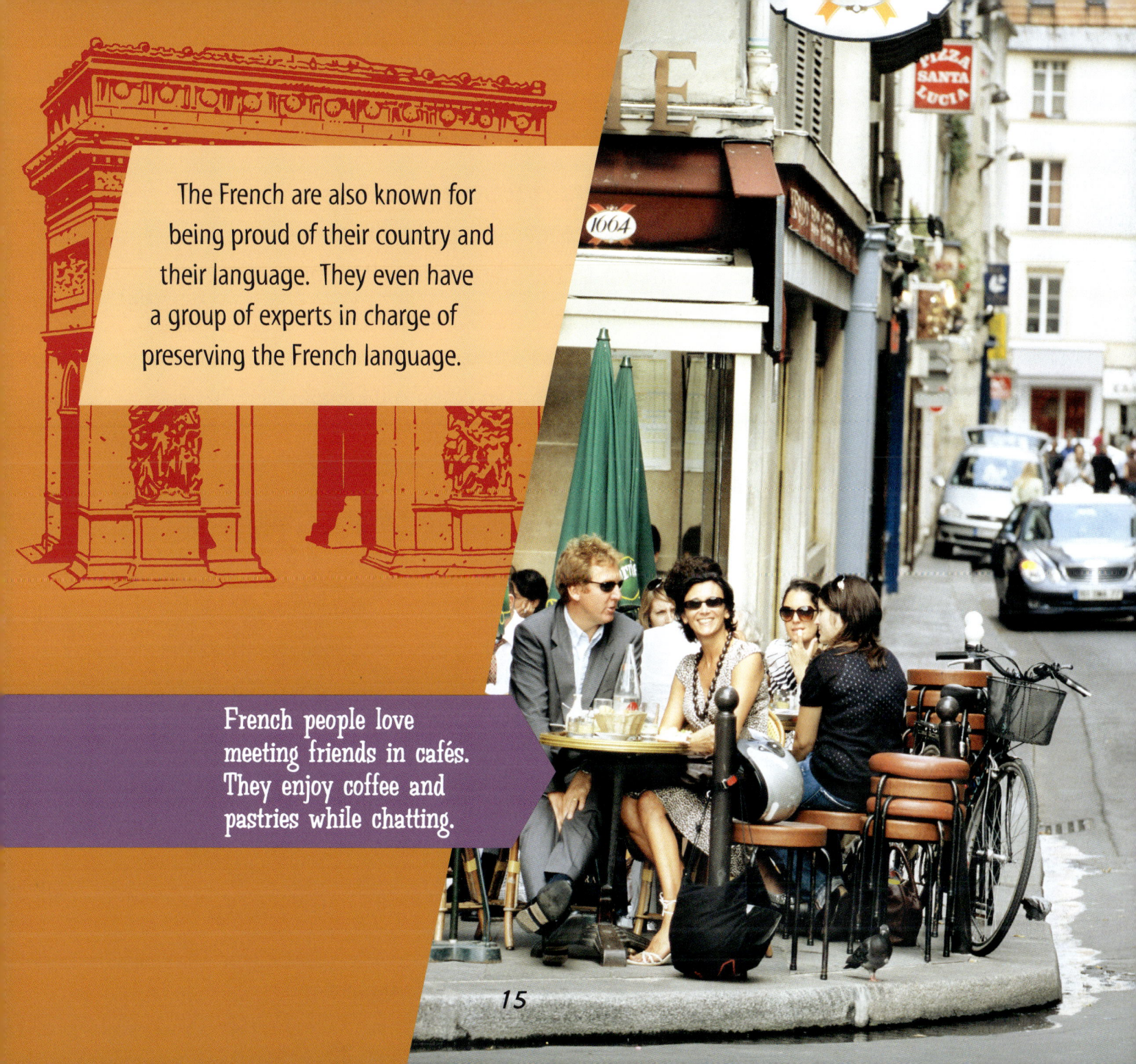

The French are also known for being proud of their country and their language. They even have a group of experts in charge of preserving the French language.

French people love meeting friends in cafés. They enjoy coffee and pastries while chatting.

Sharing Words

The French and English languages sound very different. But each has given words to the other. French has borrowed English words such as *weekend, sandwich,* and *fast food.* English has borrowed words too. Did you know that the words *dessert* and *costume* come from French?

This shop sells meat. Do you recognize any words used in English?

Talking with Hands

French people use many hand signs to help them make their point when they are speaking. Pulling on the cheek below your eye with your finger means, "I don't believe it!" Rubbing your cheek with the back of your hand means, "boring!"

French president Nicolas Sarkozy makes a gesture that means there is no room for argument.

Vœux à la presse 2006

Workers leave the subway station in Paris's business district.

Cities and Towns

Most of the French live in big cities. They often work in offices, stores, restaurants, universities, or hospitals. People bump into one another on the crowded sidewalks.

Life moves more slowly in villages. People may work on farms, in small shops or cafés, or at tourist spots. Many city families take trips to the country to enjoy the peace and quiet.

Dinard is a town in northwestern France. Shops and houses lean out over its narrow streets.

Homes

In French cities, many people live in apartments. The doorway to the building stands just a few feet from the busy street. Some old apartments are very small. They may have only two or three rooms. Newer apartments give families more space.

Apartment homes crowd together on a Paris street.

In villages, stone houses stand in rows. Sometimes they face a park at the center of town. Farmhouses in the country are bigger.

Old Homes

Some of the oldest homes in France are castles called châteaux (shah-TOH). The castles usually are built of stone. They have tall towers, many rooms, and big gardens. Rich French people lived in the castles long ago. They wanted to be safe from invaders.

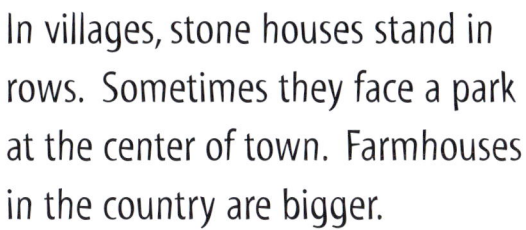

This château near the village of Chenonceaux has a large, formal garden.

These French parents have two daughters.

Family

French families used to be large. Children might have grown up with grandparents, aunts, and uncles all living under the same roof. But modern French families are smaller. Most parents have only one or two children.

A man plays with his grandchildren in a park in Paris.

All in the Family

In French, *père* means "father" and *mère* means "mother." Can you figure out what the words *grand-père* and *grand-mère* mean? *Tante* is the French word for "aunt." Can you guess what *oncle* means?

When the weather is good, French people love to eat outside. This family is on vacation in the region of Provence.

Food

Bon appétit! French people sometimes say that before a meal. They are wishing one another "good appetite!"

All over France, people enjoy long, thin, crunchy loaves of bread called baguettes. Sometimes they eat the baguettes with cheese. France is known for its many cheeses—from creamy to stinky! France also has lots of tasty desserts.

A baker removes baguettes from the oven.

And More Food!

Each area of France has its own special food. The people in eastern France like to eat snails. People who live in the northwest often eat thin pancakes called crêpes. Apples are grown in the north. They are used in cider and pastries. On the Mediterranean coast, people eat a fish stew made with fresh seafood.

A Parisian man makes crêpes on a hot griddle. Crêpes taste good with sugar, fruit, chocolate, or cheese filling.

New Foods

Have you ever eaten snails, frog legs, or sheep's brains? You might if you visited France! There, these dishes are thought of as fancy foods.

This woman is eating frog legs cooked with butter, parsley, and garlic.

Shopping

In France, shops often sell just one kind of food. You might buy bread, meat, and cheese at three different stores. Many towns also have a big outdoor market. Vegetable and fish stalls line the sidewalks. Neighbors chat as they shop.

This shop sells only vegetables. Many people buy fresh food for dinner on the way home from work every evening.

Shoppers search for old treasures in a flea market in Nice.

Some places sell expensive designer clothes. But cities also have flea markets. Sellers spread all kinds of used goods on tables or on the ground. Shoppers look for treasures.

School

In French schools, classes begin at eight or nine o'clock in the morning. They end at four or five o'clock in the afternoon. Kids get two hours for lunch! That's because most kids go home to eat with their families.

French students take a test. Does your classroom look like this?

In many places, schools are closed on Wednesdays. Students go to classes on Saturday mornings instead. Every night, kids read and do their homework.

A French girl works on her science homework.

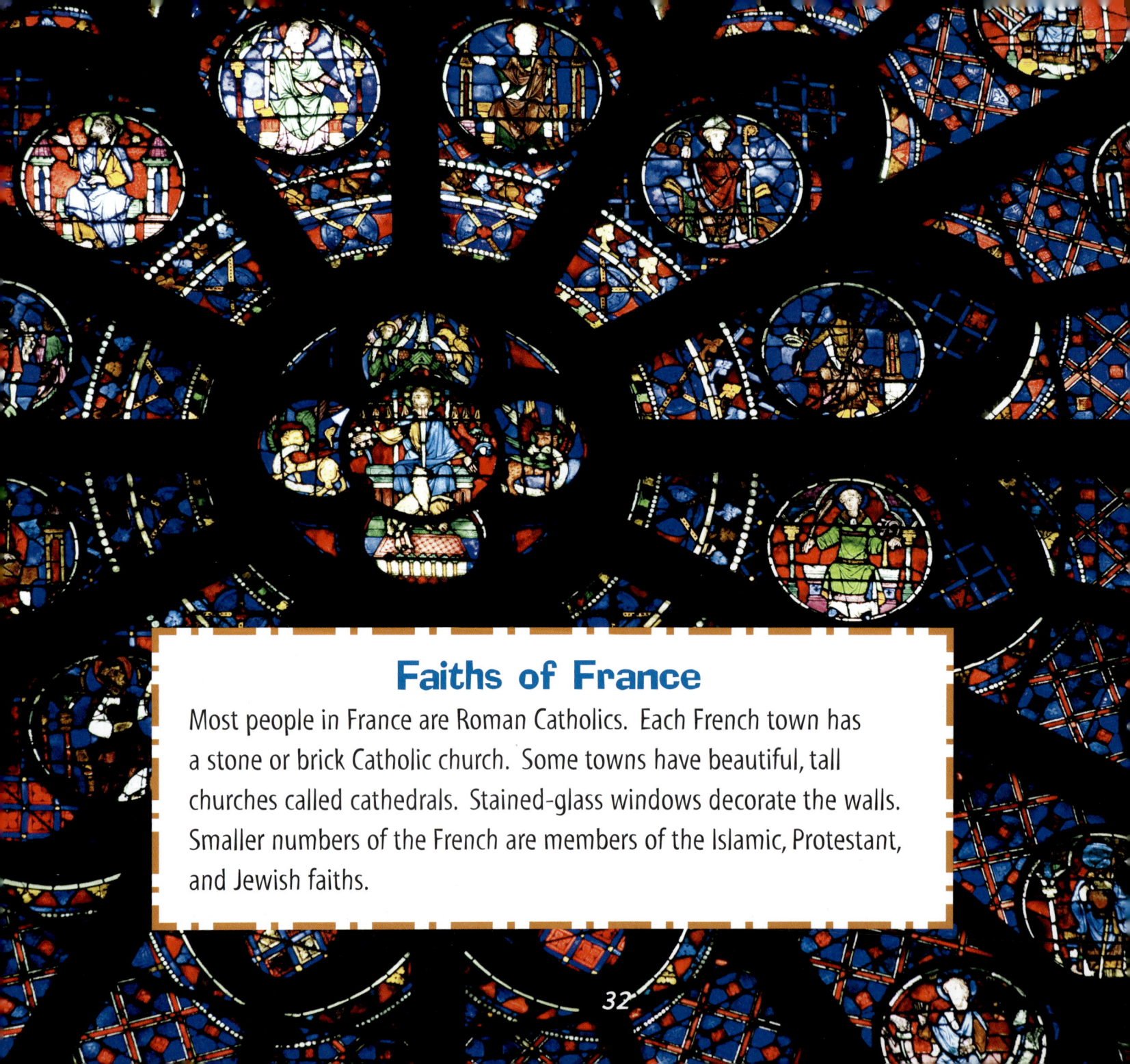

Faiths of France

Most people in France are Roman Catholics. Each French town has a stone or brick Catholic church. Some towns have beautiful, tall churches called cathedrals. Stained-glass windows decorate the walls. Smaller numbers of the French are members of the Islamic, Protestant, and Jewish faiths.

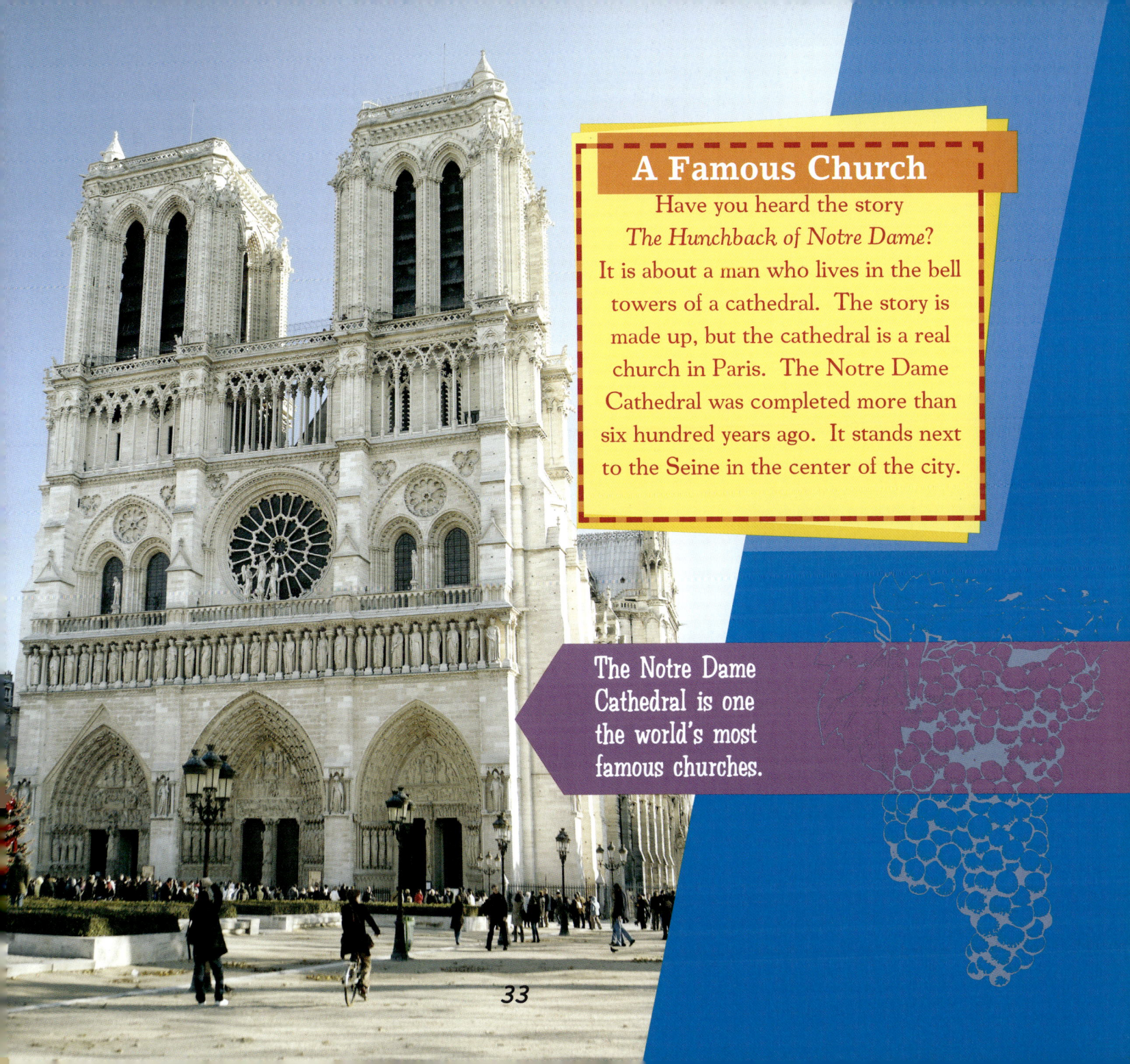

A Famous Church

Have you heard the story *The Hunchback of Notre Dame?* It is about a man who lives in the bell towers of a cathedral. The story is made up, but the cathedral is a real church in Paris. The Notre Dame Cathedral was completed more than six hundred years ago. It stands next to the Seine in the center of the city.

The Notre Dame Cathedral is one the world's most famous churches.

Let's Celebrate!

It's July 14—Bastille Day! Bastille Day is the French national holiday. It celebrates a famous attack on a prison called the Bastille. The attack helped start a revolution. French people won a larger role in their government.

Fireworks light up the Eiffel Tower during Bastille Day celebrations.

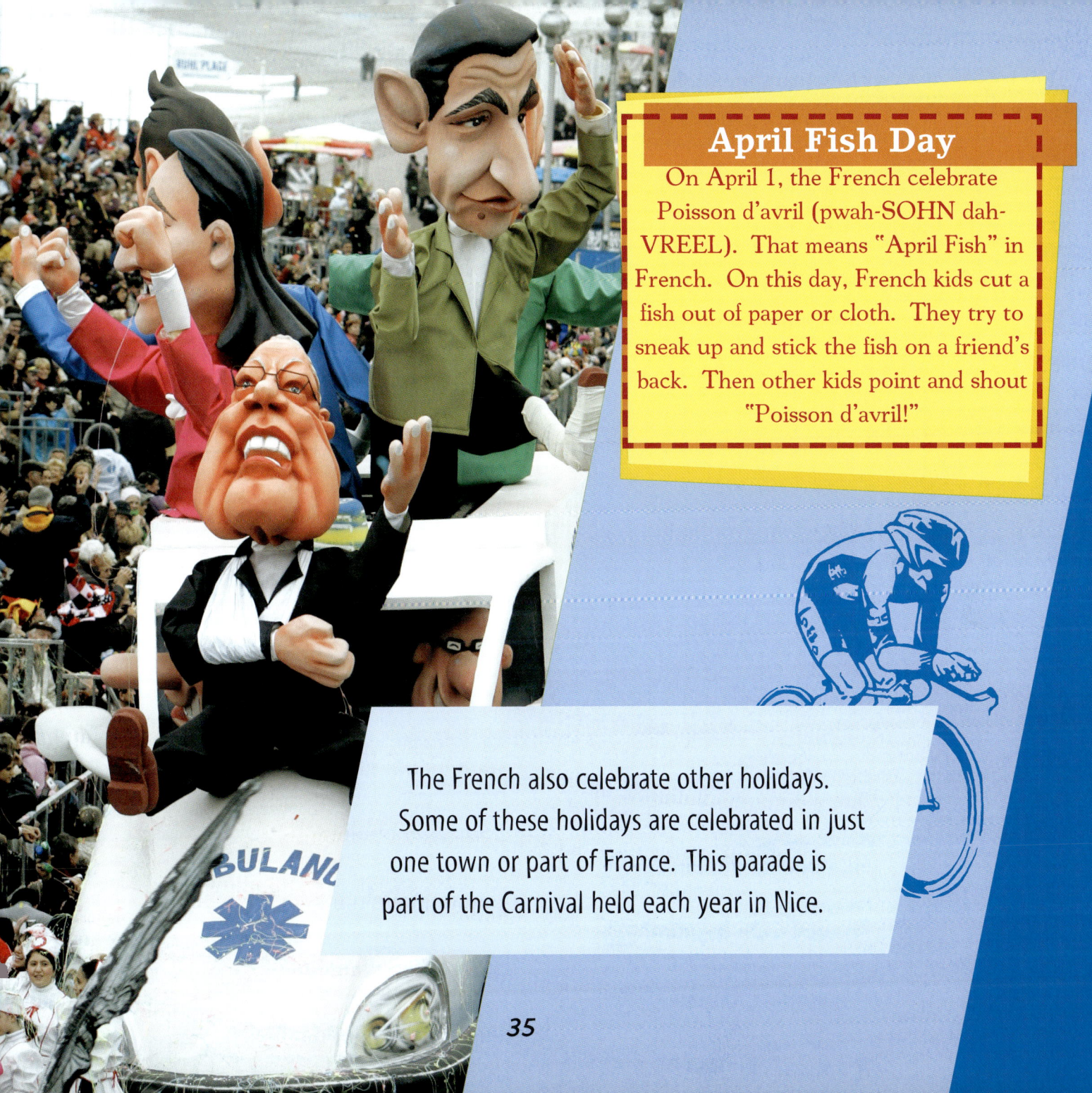

April Fish Day

On April 1, the French celebrate Poisson d'avril (pwah-SOHN dah-VREEL). That means "April Fish" in French. On this day, French kids cut a fish out of paper or cloth. They try to sneak up and stick the fish on a friend's back. Then other kids point and shout "Poisson d'avril!"

The French also celebrate other holidays. Some of these holidays are celebrated in just one town or part of France. This parade is part of the Carnival held each year in Nice.

35

Vacation

Almost everyone in France goes on vacation in August. Stores and factories close. The cities get quiet. Many families head for the beach. Some families go to the country.

The southeastern coast of France is called the French Riviera. It is one of the most famous vacation spots in the world.

Kids play soccer, tennis, or a game called *pétanque*. Some days, they fish and swim in nearby rivers. In winter, the French might go to the Alps to ski or sled.

Hi Mom! Hi Dad!

Granny and I are in the town of Bayeux. Today we went to see a long, long piece of cloth. Granny says it is called a tapestry. This cloth is the Bayeux Tapestry. It has lots of pictures that show kings and knights and fighting. It was pretty cool.

Love,
Tommy

BAYEUX TAPESTRY

On Your Bikes!

Bikes whoosh by on narrow country lanes. Motor scooters rush after them. Cars and vans follow the bikes. People stand along the roads clapping and yelling. What's all the fuss? The Tour de France!

Bicyclists race through the town of Blangy-le-Château during the Tour de France.

Near the end of the race, the Tour de France passes the Arc de Triomphe.

Every summer, bike racers from all over the world come to France. They follow a long route around the country. The race lasts three weeks. Riders go over mountains and through many towns. But the Tour de France always ends in Paris.

Story Time

French people of all ages love to read. Have you heard of *The Tales of Mother Goose?* Some of the book's stories are "Puss in Boots," "Sleeping Beauty," and "Little Red Riding Hood." A French author named Charles Perrault wrote down these tales long ago.

"Beauty and the Beast" is another fairy tale written down by a French author.

The French Academy is located in Paris.

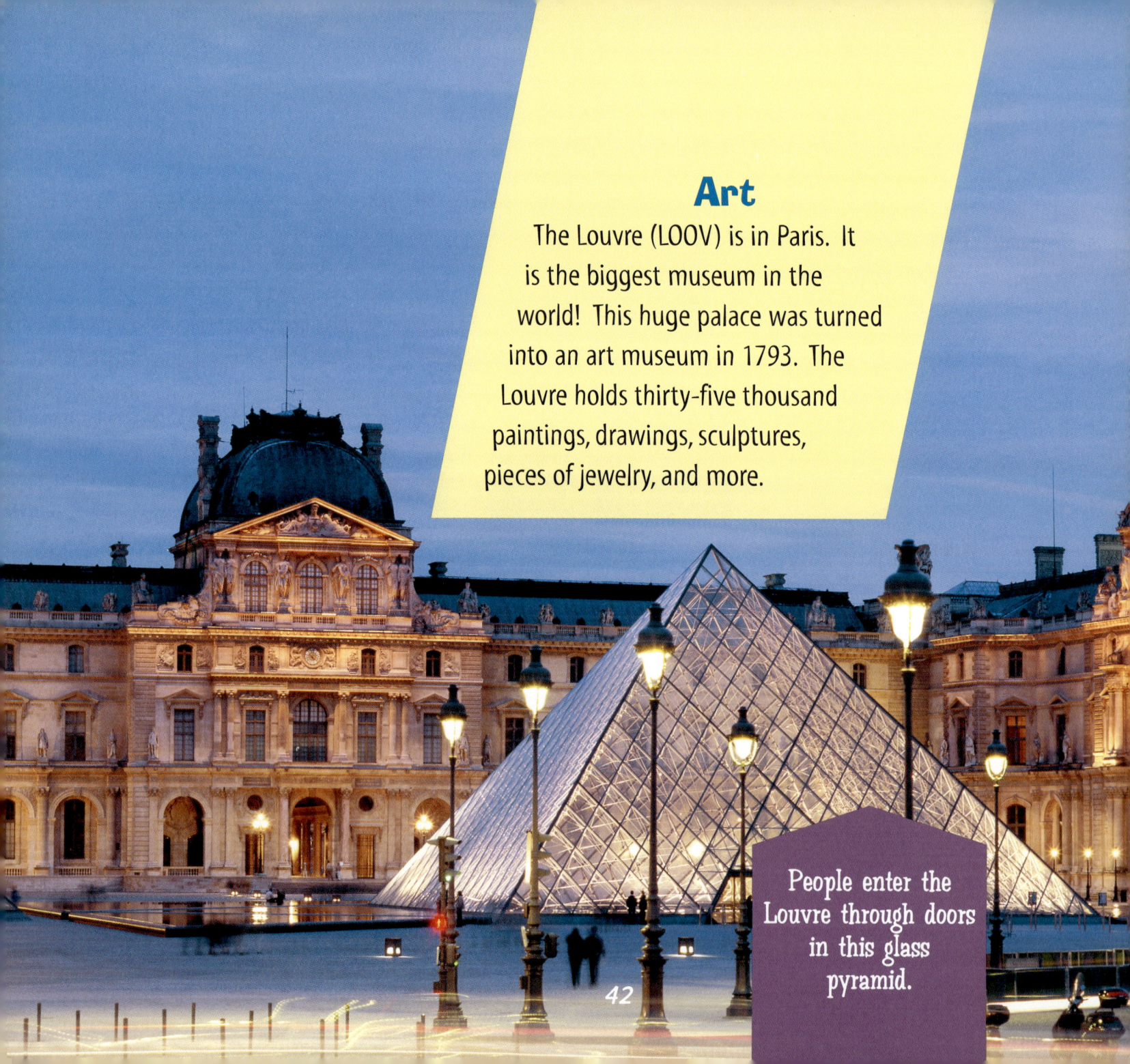

Art

The Louvre (LOOV) is in Paris. It is the biggest museum in the world! This huge palace was turned into an art museum in 1793. The Louvre holds thirty-five thousand paintings, drawings, sculptures, pieces of jewelry, and more.

People enter the Louvre through doors in this glass pyramid.

Not all art in France is in museums. One day, four French boys were looking for their dog. One boy discovered a cave. He went in and looked around. On the walls were old pictures of bulls, horses, and buffalo-like animals. The boys had found the Lascaux Caves!

The paintings in the Lascaux Caves are thousands of years old. This is one of the many horses that appear in the paintings.

THE FLAG OF FRANCE

France's flag is called the *tricolore*. That means "three-colored." The flag has a band of blue on the left, a band of red on the right, and white in the middle. Blue and red were once the colors of Paris. White stood for the king. The three colors were first used together in 1789, soon after the storming of the Bastille. The colors showed that the people of France were joined together in the French Revolution. Several years later, the tricolore became the French flag.

FAST FACTS

FULL COUNTRY NAME: French Republic

AREA: 211,208 square miles (547,030 square kilometers). That is about twice as big as the state of Colorado.

MAIN LANDFORMS: the mountain ranges Alps, Jura, and Pyrenees; the plateau Massif Central; the wetlands, the Camargue

MAJOR RIVERS: Loire, Rhône, Seine

ANIMALS AND THEIR HABITATS: badgers (forests, grassy or sandy areas); boars (forests and fields); brown bears, chamois, ibex (mountains); deer, foxes, lynx, rabbits (forests); flamingos, horses, wild bulls (Camargue wetlands); wall lizard (throughout France)

CAPITAL CITY: Paris

OFFICIAL LANGUAGE: French

POPULATION: about 60,876,136

GLOSSARY

ancestors: relatives who lived long ago

appetite: desire to eat. French people say, "Bon appétit!" to wish one another a good appetite, or a good meal.

baguette: a long, skinny, crispy loaf of bread that is common in France

canal: a waterway made by humans to link rivers to one another

capital: a city where the government is located

cathedral: a large, often fancy church

cave: a natural space underground

châteaux: old castles in France, usually made of stone

continent: any one of seven large areas of land. The continents are Africa, Antarctica, Asia, Australia, Europe, North America, and South America.

expert: someone who knows a lot about a certain subject

ibex: a wild goat

plateau: an area of high, flat land

preserving: protecting from unwanted change

revolution: a violent uprising by a country's people that changes the system of government

TO LEARN MORE

BOOKS

Fisher, Teresa. *France.* Food and Festivals series. Austin, TX: Raintree Steck-Vaughn, 1999. Find out more about French foods in this book.

Haskins, Jim, and Kathleen Benson. *Count Your Way through France.* Minneapolis: Carolrhoda Books, 1996. Learn how to count to ten in French.

Haviland, Virginia. *Favorite Fairy Tales Told in France.* New York: Beech Tree Books, 1994. This book includes "Beauty and the Beast" and other stories from France.

Munro, Roxie. *The Inside-Outside Book of Paris.* New York: Dutton Children's Books, 1992. Check out the sights of Paris in this illustrated book.

Waldee, Lynne Marie. *Cooking the French Way.* Minneapolis: Lerner Publications, 2002. Use these recipes to try cooking some French favorites!

WEBSITES

France
http://www.timeforkids.com/TFK/kids/hh/goplaces/main/0,28375,491045,00.html
This website from the magazine *Time for Kids* features virtual tours of France, a guide to French phrases, a quiz about France, and more.

INDEX

art, 42–43

city life, 8, 11, 18, 20
country life, 10, 19, 21

families, 22–23
food, 16, 24–27

holidays, 34–35
homes, 20–21

language, 15, 16–17, 23, 41

map of France, 5

people, 12–15, 22

religion, 32–33

schools, 30–31
sports, 37

vacation, 36–37

The photographs in this book are used with the permission of: © Steve Vidler/SuperStock, pp. 4, 14; © Photononstop/SuperStock, pp. 6, 21; © iStockphoto.com/Kelly Borsheim, p. 7; © Charles Jean Marc/CORBIS SYGMA, p. 8; © iStockphoto.com, p. 9; © David Crossland/Alamy, p. 10; AP Photo/Claude Paris, p. 11; AP Photo/Bob Edme, p. 12; © Mark Henley/Panos Pictures, p. 13; © Dieter Telemans/Panos Pictures, p. 15; © Kevin Galvin/Alamy, p. 16; AP Photo/Francois Mori, pp. 17, 18, 34; © Nicole Duplaix/National Geographic/Getty Images, p. 19; © Iksung Nah/Alamy, p. 20; © Erin Patrice O'Brien/Taxi/Getty Images, p. 22; © Jonathan Smith/Lonely Planet Images, p. 23; © Nick Hanna/Alamy, p. 24; © age fotostock/SuperStock, pp. 25, 42; © AA World Travel Library/Alamy, p. 26; © Emmanuel Lattes/Alamy, p. 27; © Art Kowalsky/Alamy, p. 28; © Robert Harding Picture Library Ltd/Alamy, p. 29; © Alex Bartel/Art Directors, p. 30; © Philippe Lissac/Godong/CORBIS, p. 31; © iStockphoto.com/Bill Fowle, p. 32; © iStockphoto.com/David Lentz, p. 33; AP Photo/Lionel Cironneau, p. 35; © Gavin Hellier/Alamy, p. 36; © INTERFOTO Pressebildagentur/Alamy, p. 37; AP Photo/Peter Dejong, pp. 38, 39; © Pictorial Press Ltd/Alamy, p. 40; © Laurent Houdayer/AFP/Getty Images, p. 41; © SuperStock Inc./SuperStock, p. 43. Illustrations by © Bill Hauser/Independent Picture Service.

Cover: © Todd Gipstein/National Geographic/Getty Images